T0368506

Mommy and Me, When Mommy is Away

K. Jody Massey

WestBow Press books may be ordered through booksellers or by contacting:

WestBow Press
A Division of Thomas Nelson & Zondervan
1663 Liberty Drive
Bloomington, IN 47403
www.westbowpress.com
844-714-3454

ISBN: 979-8-3850-2752-1 (sc)
ISBN: 979-8-3850-2753-8 (hc)
ISBN: 979-8-3850-2754-5 (e)

Library of Congress Control Number: 2024912057

Print information available on the last page.

WestBow Press rev. date: 10/04/2024

WESTBOW
PRESS®
A DIVISION OF THOMAS NELSON
& ZONDERVAN

THIS BOOK
BELONGS TO:

_____

My sweet child, I made choices that took me away from you.

Mommy, May I ask you a question?

What *do* you *do* when you are away?

My sweet child, I do the same things you do.

Even though we are apart, you are aways in my heart!

We both see the rain.

We both see the sun.

HOPE

GRACE

JOY

MERCY

PEACE

FREEDOM

REFUGE

COMFORT

7

We both run and
like to have fun!

We both get sad.
We both get mad.

10

When it is night, I wish
I could hold you tight!

The hardest thing I do
is be away from you.

12

Out of all
the things I do,

I mostly

LOVE

to see you!

To all who read this book,
You are worthy of a wonderful life full of abundant love,
grace and forgiveness. You are Special!
You are Unique! There is only one YOU!
Your life has a purpose that only you can fulfill.
No matter what mistakes have been made,
there is always HOPE!
The hope of joy
The hope of peace
The hope of victory
The hope of rescue
The hope of living without guilt and shame
The hope of restoration
The hope of loving yourself
The hope of a new beginning
There is nothing you could ever do to keep you from
receiving all these things.

Questions You and Your Child Can Discuss

When will I *see* you again?

How long will you be gone?

Can I call you?

Can I email you?

Can I text you?

Can I *see* you every week?

Why did you leave me?

Do you love me?

Do you know how much I love you, Mommy?

Do you miss me?

Do you know how much I miss you, Mommy?

What did you *do* to get taken away from me?

Who took you away?

Why did the police take you away?

Is this the Policeman's fault?

Is this my fault?

GRATEFULNESS

I am so very grateful to share this book with
you! God gave me the heart, the life experiences
and every word to write this book. No matter
the circumstances, I believe every child deserves
to know they are loved by their parent.

My heart is so thankful for all that God has provided
for this book. He has given me the most loving and
encouraging husband. His divine favor led me to my Editor,
Dr. Cathy Block. Their constant love and guidance has
encouraged me to do His work and I am forever thankful for
them! I am also grateful for all the endless prayers and
support from my family and my Sisters in Christ.

-K. Jody Massey

Printed in the United States
by Baker & Taylor Publisher Services

This book is designed to bring hope and nurturing to the relationship between a child and a parent that is away from home.

There are many reasons for a child/parent separation... incarceration, substance abuse rehabilitation, foster care, divorce, military duty or long distance work assignments. This book can assist in building a stronger parent/child connection in any situation in which a parent simply can't care for her child on a daily basis.

We hope this book builds children's understanding of the deep love their parents have for them.

"Any journey that separates a parent and child is never an easy journey for one to travel. However, K. Jody Massey has created a simple way to close this difficult gap. The Daddy and Me & Mommy and Me children's books can help the child know and believe that although they are out of sight they are never out of mind."
- **Andre L. Johnson**, Director, Reentry Services, Reentry First Stop Center for Tarrant County, Fort Worth, TX

WESTBOW PRESS®
A DIVISION OF THOMAS NELSON & ZONDERVAN

U.S.
ISBN 979-8-3850-2752-

5129

9 798385 027521